THE ARMENIAN EARTHQUAKE

Look for these and other exciting
World Disasters books:

Pompeii
The Black Death
The Titanic
The Chicago Fire
The San Francisco Earthquake
The Crash of '29
The Dust Bowl

THE
ARMENIAN
EARTHQUAKE

by
Chris Engholm

Illustrations by Maurie Manning
and
Michael Spackman
Robert Caldwell
Randol Eagles

LUCENT
B·O·O·K·S

WORLD DISASTERS

Library of Congress Cataloging-in-Publication Data
Engholm, Christopher, 1969-
    The Armenian earthquake / by Christopher Engholm;
illustrations by Maurie Manning.
      p.   cm. — (World disasters)
    Bibliography: p.
    Includes index.
    Summary: Describes the Armenian earthquake of 1988 and its historical, political and cultural aspects.
    1-56006-004-2
    1. Armenian S.S.R.—History—Juvenile literature. 2. Earthquakes—
Armenian S.S.R.—Juvenile literature.   [1.Earthquakes—Armenian S.S.R.
2.Armenian S.S.R.—History.] I. Manning, Maurie 1960- ill. II. Title III. Series.
DK687.E54 1989
956.6'2038—dc20   89-33555
                                                          CIP
                                                            AC

For Elizabeth Wehmeyer

Table of Contents

Preface
The World Disasters Series

World disasters have always aroused human curiosity. Whenever news of tragedy spreads, we want to learn more about it. We wonder how and why the disaster happened, how people reacted, and whether we might have acted differently. To be sure, disaster evokes a wide range of responses—fear, sorrow, despair, generosity, even hope. Yet from every great disaster, one remarkable truth always seems to emerge: in spite of death, pain, and destruction, the human spirit triumphs.

History is full of great disasters, which arise from a variety of causes. Earthquakes, floods, volcanic eruptions, and other natural events often produce widespread destruction. Just as often, however, people accidentally bring suffering and distress on themselves and other human beings. And many disasters have sinister causes, like human greed, envy, or prejudice.

The disasters included in this series have been chosen not only for their dramatic qualities, but also for their educational value. The reader will learn about the causes and effects of the greatest disasters in history. Technical concepts and interesting anecdotes are explained and illustrated in inset boxes.

But disasters should not be viewed in isolation. To enrich the reader's understanding, these books present historical information about the time period, and interesting facts about the culture in which each disaster occurred. Finally, they teach valuable lessons about human nature. More acts of bravery, cowardice, intelligence, and foolishness are compressed into the few days of a disaster than most people experience in a lifetime.

Dramatic illustrations and evocative narrative lure the reader to distant cities and times gone by. Readers witness the awesome power of an exploding volcano, the magnitude of a violent earthquake, and the hopelessness of passengers on a mighty ship passing to its watery grave. By reliving the events, the reader will see how disaster affects the lives of real people and will gain a deeper understanding of their sorrow, their pain, their courage, and their hope.

Introduction
The Evil Beneath the Surface

In the mountains of southwest Asia, between the Black Sea and the Caspian Sea, lies the country of Armenia. Thousands of years ago, the people of Armenia founded one of the earliest civilizations in this part of the world. Throughout their history, they have been an industrious and, for the most part, prosperous people. However, their picturesque cities with ancient temples, churches, and traditional one-story stone houses only tell part of the story of Armenia's past.

The other part is one of the darkest and most troubling histories of any nation, culture, or race in the world. As a small but prosperous nation, Armenia was the target of one foreign takeover after another. Often, this foreign control was enforced violently, but never more violently than during the twenty year period between 1895 and 1915. At that time, Armenia was struggling to win its independence from the Turkish Ottoman Empire. To put down this threat to their empire, Turkish soldiers killed approximately one million Armenian men, women, and children.

Armenia is no longer ruled by Turks. Since 1920, it has been part of the Soviet Union, but the anguish of its past and the distrust of foreign rulers has not been forgotten. The Armenian people take great pride in their history, but it also gives them reason to fear.

Ironically, what is true of Armenia's history is also true of the land itself. In Armenia's landscape, there is much to marvel at, but beneath the surface, there is much to fear. Many of Armenia's cities are nestled in meadows and mountain valleys. Others are silhouetted against rugged canyons and steep mountains. Although striking in their beauty, these jagged ridges and mountains are evidence of great disturbances beneath the earth's surface. The rocky, mountainous landscape of Armenia has been formed by violent movements of the earth's crust, movements that we know as earthquakes.

Every year, the country is shaken by hundreds of minor earthquakes. But on December 7, 1988, a devastating earthquake, centered in northern Armenia between the cities of Spitak and Stepanavan, rocked the country. These and other cities, along with hundreds of villages, were completely leveled. More than twenty-five thousand people were killed.

Yet once again, the statistics tell only part of the story. The earthquake was a natural disaster, but the tragic loss of lives and property was greatly increased by human mistakes and miscalculations. Placing the blame for these errors triggered divisions among Armenians, Russians, and other peoples of the region. Many old political wounds were reopened. That is why the story of the Armenian earthquake of 1988 is not just a story of a natural disaster, but of a proud people who look back on a troubled past.

The Armenian Earthquake's Place in History

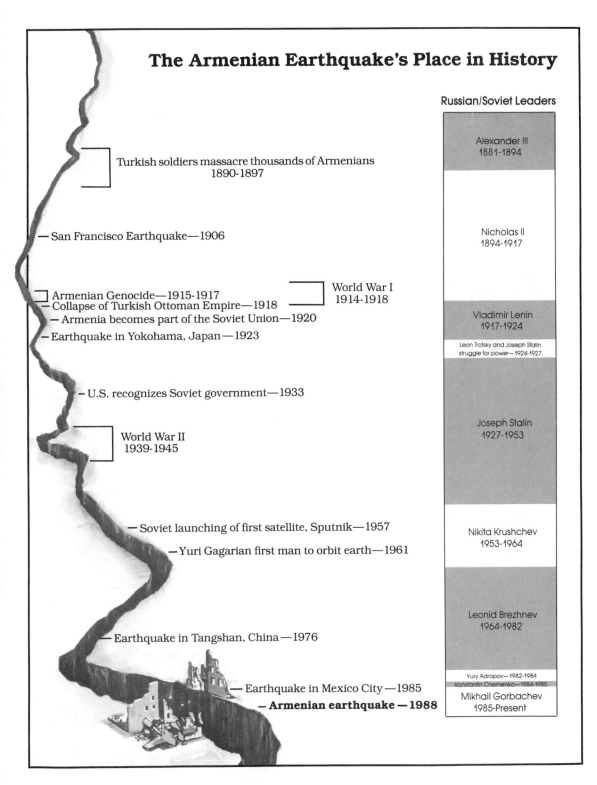

Russian/Soviet Leaders

Alexander III
1881-1894

Nicholas II
1894-1917

Vladimir Lenin
1917-1924

Leon Trotsky and Joseph Stalin
struggle for power—1924-1927

Joseph Stalin
1927-1953

Nikita Krushchev
1953-1964

Leonid Brezhnev
1964-1982

Yury Adropov—1982-1984
Konstantin Chernenko—1984-1985
Mikhail Gorbachev
1985-Present

Turkish soldiers massacre thousands of Armenians
1890-1897

San Francisco Earthquake—1906

Armenian Genocide—1915-1917
Collapse of Turkish Ottoman Empire—1918
Armenia becomes part of the Soviet Union—1920
Earthquake in Yokohama, Japan—1923

World War I
1914-1918

U.S. recognizes Soviet government—1933

World War II
1939-1945

Soviet launching of first satellite, Sputnik—1957

Yuri Gagarian first man to orbit earth—1961

Earthquake in Tangshan, China—1976

Earthquake in Mexico City—1985
Armenian earthquake—1988

One
A Troubled Past

In the early 1800s, the great Russian writer, Aleksandr Pushkin, wrote that Armenia was filled with "fertile, green fields." Pushkin had entered the country from the northeast and had descended "the gentle mountain slope to the fresh plains of Armenia."

In 1919, an Englishman named H. Lynch entered the country farther to the south, near the city of Leninaken, and wrote that Armenia was full of "knolls and hills" and "mountain masses which changed their colors with every change in the sky."

A third picture was painted a decade later by a Russian botanist who had spent time in the Ararat Valley near the country's present capital, Yerevan. He wrote that Armenia was a dry, salt-covered plateau, dotted with ancient temples, resembling the deserts of Arabia and Egypt.

All of these descriptions are accurate, but each one describes only a single region of Armenia. This **republic** is part of the USSR (Union of Soviet Socialist Republics) and is only the size of Maryland. Yet it contains a variety of landscapes and climates that one would not expect in such a small country.

Although the landscape varies greatly, one invisible feature ties all of Armenia to a common fate. Armenia is earthquake country. Long cracks, or **faults**, in the earth's **crust**, crisscross Armenia. In most places, these faults lie only about 15 miles (24 kilometers) below ground level. The earth's crust is known to shift along these shallow faults. In fact, the mountainous landscape where most Armenians live shifts frequently. And whenever it shifts, an earthquake occurs.

Over the past five hundred years, Armenia has endured hundreds of earthquakes. Fifteen of them have been strong enough to cause serious damage. In 1926, a powerful quake shook the earth so violently that six thousand homes collapsed, killing thousands of people.

Armenia's long history of earthquakes parallels a history of political upheaval. Often in Armenia's past, nature and politics have combined to deal this small country one tragic blow after another.

When they first settled in the mountains west of the Caspian Sea over twenty-five hundred years ago, Armenians established one of the earliest civilizations in this part of the world. They had **migrated** to this area from the Mediterranean region. That is why most Armenians have the black hair and olive skin characteristic of Mediterranean peoples.

Throughout their history, Armenians have been known as an industrious and prosperous people. Unfortunately, their population has never been very large, and their prosperity has often made them the target of foreign empires. As a result, Armenia has been ruled by foreign conquerors for most of the past two thousand years.

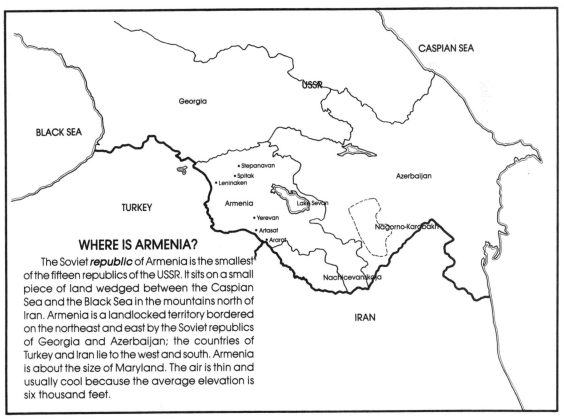

WHERE IS ARMENIA?

The Soviet *republic* of Armenia is the smallest of the fifteen republics of the USSR. It sits on a small piece of land wedged between the Caspian Sea and the Black Sea in the mountains north of Iran. Armenia is a landlocked territory bordered on the northeast and east by the Soviet republics of Georgia and Azerbaijan; the countries of Turkey and Iran lie to the west and south. Armenia is about the size of Maryland. The air is thin and usually cool because the average elevation is six thousand feet.

12

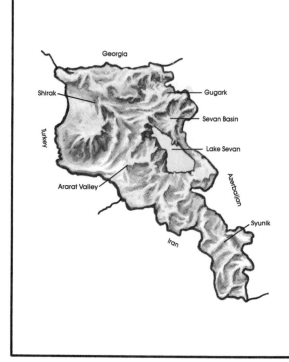

A COUNTRY OF STONES

The Soviet republic of Armenia is made up mostly of volcanic rock which began forming over a billion years ago. In fact, one-third of the country is covered with rocks, and Armenians themselves refer to their land as Ayastan-Karastan, the "country of stones."

Armenia, a land of mountain ranges and lowlands, is divided into five regions. The Ararat Valley (see map) is covered with fruit orchards and plantations. The bountiful Shirak region boasts of abundant grain fields and green mountain slopes dotted with countless flocks of sheep. To the northeast lies the mountainous Gugark region with its copper mines and chemical factories. The Sevan Basin features Lake Sevan, the republic's largest lake, known for excellent fishing. South of Lake Sevan is the nearly inaccessible mountain region known as Syunik. A picturesque land, Syunik is home to sculpted rock formations, natural tunnels, raging rivers, and huge waterfalls.

From the fifteenth through the nineteenth centuries, this small nation controlled the trade of silk, cotton, wool, and carpets throughout Asia Minor. During this time, Armenia was ruled by the powerful Turkish Ottoman Empire. Yet Armenians preserved their national identity with fierce pride. This they achieved by remaining firmly tied to family and religious traditions. The tradition of large, close-knit families has helped keep the Armenian culture alive. In the past, grandparents, aunts, uncles, parents, and children all lived together in groups that often exceeded sixty family members. These families gathered together to attend Armenian churches, celebrate holidays, sing folk songs, and tell folktales that recall their centuries of suffering.

Since 1920, Armenia has been one of the fifteen republics ruled by the USSR, or Soviet Union. Along with the republics of Azerbaijan and Georgia, it covers the mountainous region that lies between Turkey and the Caspian Sea in

the southwest corner of the Soviet Union.

Before 1920, these republics were either independent countries or ruled by other, more powerful nations. Since then, Soviet leaders have worked to unify the people of these countries into a single nation. However, language, economics, religion, and social customs have divided these people for hundreds of years. The Soviet leaders are trying to make these people overlook centuries of rivalry and hatred.

For example, the Armenians and Azerbaijanis have been feuding for years over a strip of land called the Nagorno-Karabakh Autonomous Region. The region lies inside Azerbaijan's borders and is governed by Azerbaijanis. Most Azerbaijanis belong to the Muslim religion, but the Nagorno-Karabakh is populated almost entirely by Christian Armenians —over 180,000 of them. Most Armenians feel the region was forcibly taken from them by the Soviet Union in the early 1900s, and they want it back.

In February 1988, Armenian workers living in Nagorno-Karabakh went on strike as a way to show their dislike of Azerbaijani rule. Meanwhile, in the Armenian capital of Yerevan, hundreds of thousands of Armenians demonstrated in the streets against Azerbaijani rule of the Nagorno-Karabakh. On a few occasions, violent riots have broken out. Soviet troops have even opened fire on crowds of Armenians who attacked troops with bricks and pipes.

ARMENIA'S CONQUERORS

Throughout much of its history, Armenia has been a conquered land. In 519 BC, the country was successfully invaded from the south by **Persian** armies. Alexander the Great, the famous **Macedonian** ruler, occupied Armenia in 334 BC. In 628 AD, Armenia became part of the **Byzantine Empire**, and was ruled from **Constantinople** by a foreign emperor. Only twenty-five years later it was again conquered, this time by Arabs.

For the past one thousand years, Armenia has continued to be conquered and ruled by foreign powers, including **Mongols** and Turks. From about 1500 to 1918, Armenia was ruled by the Ottoman Turks whose capital was in Constantinople. Finally, in December, 1920, it was proclaimed a Soviet republic by the Armenian Communist party.

The conflict between Armenia and Azerbaijan has deep roots. Its origin lies in the tragic past shared by the two peoples. The Azerbaijanis are Turkish by descent. And it was under the rule of the Turkish Ottoman Empire that Armenians suffered the terrible massacres known as the Armenian *genocide*.

Turkish *oppression* of Armenia began in the mid 1800s in the form of heavy taxes. Many Armenians longed for independence from the Turkish *regime*, but they did not have the strength to rebel against the powerful Turks. In 1877, however, the Turks went to war with Russia. Today Russia is part of the USSR, but at that time it was an independent nation. In its war against Turkey, most Armenians supported Russia.

When Turkey was defeated by Russia, many Armenians experienced the wrath of the Turkish army. Suspecting all Armenians of siding with the Russians, the Turks began searching Armenian homes and arresting people they accused of plotting against the Turkish government. Most of those arrested were executed. By 1895, the Turks had killed more than three hundred thousand Armenian men, women, and children.

The massacre was intended to halt the Armenian independence movement. Instead, it aroused such anger that Armenians were more united than ever. They formed the Armenian National Movement, which waged *guerrilla* attacks on the Turkish army. For the first

THE CHURCH IN ARMENIA

In 300 AD, Armenia became the first nation to embrace Christianity. According to legend, Noah's Ark washed ashore on Mt. Ararat in Armenia. In fact, the name of Armenia's capital, Yerevan, comes from the word *ereval*, which means "it appears." These were the words Noah shouted when he first spied land after the biblical flood.

Today, although the current Soviet government tends to discourage churchgoing in the Soviet Union, most Armenians openly practice their religion. The majority of Armenians belong to either the Apostolic Church, the Catholic Church, or the Protestant Church. Because Armenians continue to practice religion against the government's wishes, religious worship has become a symbol of Armenian individuality and independence.

time in over six centuries, a large number of Armenians cried out for self-rule.

But they were pitifully outnumbered and had no chance against the Turks—until 1914. Then World War I broke out, and once again, Armenia became a battleground for Russian and Turkish troops. The results were the same as they had been in 1878. The Russians defeated the Turks, and the Turks blamed their loss on the disloyalty of the Armenians.

This time, Turkish brutality made the massacre of 1895 seem slight by comparison. Even Armenian soldiers who had fought for the Turks were massacred. First, they were forced to march hundreds of miles, carrying heavy loads through snow-covered mountains from Armenia to **Constantinople**. Those who fell and refused to go on were whipped or jabbed with bayonets. Men too exhausted to continue were left to die. Many of those who survived until they reached their destination were executed.

Turkish soldiers also raided Armenian towns and villages. They captured fifty or a hundred Armenian soldiers, tied them together in groups of four, and marched them to a secluded spot outside the village. Then the sound of rifle shots was heard in the village as the bound soldiers were killed.

Turkish authorities tore up Armenian homes searching for hidden weapons. They killed men, women, and even children whom they accused of conspiring against the Turkish government. They suspected the Armenian church of encouraging rebellion. After ransacking the churches and beating priests until they were unconscious, soldiers held rude ceremonies that mocked Christian church services.

Armenian women were sometimes forced to marry Muslim men on demand. Many refused, even though they were often carried into the hills and killed. Babies were left on the ground to die or were hurled against the rocks. In 1915 alone, more than 1.5 million Armenians were slain. Of the 2.5 million Armenians about 1 million were left.

Not all Turks approved of the genocide. Some protected Armenian families by hiding them in their basements and cellars. Others brought them food and clothing so they could remain in hiding. Some Turks even adopted orphaned Armenian children and cared for them as their own.

Unfortunately, most Armenians had seen so much suffering that they did not trust any Turks. They suspected that the adoption of Armenian children was another way to eliminate their culture and heritage. After the genocide, thousands of Armenians left their homeland to find safer places to live. By the end of World War I in 1917, over seventy thousand Armenian people had arrived in the United States.

After World War I, the Turkish Ottoman Empire was dismantled. In 1918, Armenia declared itself an independent nation. This was the first time

in over four hundred years that Armenia had achieved self-rule. But its independence lasted less than a year.

The Russian Revolution had taken place in 1917, and Russia began to exert its power in the region. A year later, Vladimir Lenin and other Russian leaders of the Communist party established the government of the Union of Soviet Socialist Republics in Moscow. In 1919, the Soviet Red Army, composed mainly of Russian troops, took control of Armenia. On November 29, 1920, the Soviet government formed the Armenian Soviet Socialist Republic, making Armenia one of fifteen Soviet republics.

Although Armenia had its own government, which was controlled by the Communist party, the power to control Armenia's economy, school system, and defense was held by the central government in Moscow.

Armenian resentment toward Russia and the Soviet government grew until Armenian **nationalists** attempted a revolt in 1921. Within days, the revolt was crushed by the powerful Red Army.

The Soviet leader at the time, Joseph Stalin, tried to win the cooperation of Armenia and other non-Russian republics that had rebelled. He offered these republics the right to use their own national languages and practice their traditional customs.

By 1930, however, resistance to Russian control was becoming increasingly violent throughout the Soviet Union. To discourage rebellion, Stalin **purged** non-Russian intellectuals from the Communist party. Anyone who showed the slightest interest in non-Russian nationalism was accused of treason. Thousands of Armenian intellectuals were imprisoned or killed, including some of the country's most famous writers.

Then Stalin condemned the minority cultures, including the Armenian culture, as anti-Russian. The schools in every republic were required to teach the Russian alphabet and language so that expressions of Armenian and other non-Russian cultures were discouraged. Folk songs, poetry, and operas in **ethnic** languages were banned. By law, everyone was required to speak Russian. Stalin became known as "the man of steel" and declared that the Russian people would lead the other peoples of the Soviet Union into the future.

Stalin's tyranny lasted until the late 1950s. Since then, his successors have gradually restored many minority rights and encouraged the non-Russian republics to become more productive. After years of stagnation, the Armenian economy began to flourish once again.

Since 1985, under the leadership of Mikhail Gorbachev, the Soviet Union has begun a new policy of **glasnost**, or openness. Armenians and other Soviet citizens have been granted greater freedom to speak their minds. They can publish their own newspapers and communicate freely with relatives living abroad.

This newfound freedom has not come without difficulties, however. For years, Armenians had to suppress their national pride, their anger over Nagorno-Karabakh, and their disagreements with the ruling Communist party. But all this time, Armenian resentment and distrust of the Soviets simmered just beneath the surface. Ironically, the greater freedoms introduced by Gorbachev allowed the Armenians to lift the lid on their resentment. Years of suppressed anger boiled over on the streets of Armenian cities, where people demonstrated in favor of **annexing** Nagorno-Karabakh. Once again, they spoke freely about their dream of self-rule.

This was the political landscape of Armenia in December 1988. On the surface, things were still tranquil, but a history of conflict and ill will lurked just beneath the surface. No one could predict what events might bring these conflicts into the open. But as the Armenian people had learned to expect, soon something would happen to shatter their uneasy peace.

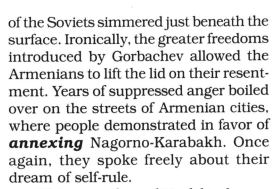

ARMENIANS THROUGHOUT THE WORLD

Many Armenians who survived the **genocide** of 1915 left their country to find safety in other parts of the world. In 1916 and 1917, they began arriving by ship in France, England, the United States, and many other countries. By 1917, over seventy thousand Armenians had arrived in the United States.

In the U.S., the Armenians proved to be extremely enterprising. Although most came with very little money, they adapted quickly to the language and customs of their new home. They learned English and started working as barbers, bakers, carpenters, teachers, lawyers, tailors, weavers, and clergymen.

At present, nearly four million Armenians are scattered throughout the world. This wide dispersion of Armenians is called the Armenian **diaspora**, from a Greek word meaning to scatter, or sow like seeds. Proud of their heritage, the "scattered" Armenian people continue to practice their old ethnic traditions in their adopted countries.

Two
An Uneasy Peace

Since Armenia came under Russian control in 1920, traditional Armenian culture, customs, and religion have merged with the faster-paced, urban lifestyle of modern Russia. In many ways, the mix has been a successful one. The hard work of the Armenian people has helped the republic to prosper. Their products, such as electrical appliances, fine wines, and clothing, are sold around the world.

Yet everywhere, the duel between these two cultures is evident. Ancient architecture and traditional customs compete with the stark surroundings of a modern, industrial state. The Ararat Valley, where the capital city of Yerevan is located, is dotted with ancient cities, such as Armavir, Artashat, Vagharshapat, and Dvin. Ancient temples, pagan fortresses, and cave monasteries have been standing in these cities for centuries. Everywhere, the Armenians have erected monuments and statues honoring heroes of the past. In fact, there are so many outdoor monuments, ruins, and old churches that the country has been called an open-air museum.

Right alongside these ancient monuments stand high-tech factories, high-rise apartment buildings, and, in the countryside, modern farm machinery. The contrasts between old and new are often most obvious in country villages. These villages usually lie on the fertile lands where rivers flow out of the mountains and into the valleys. A village is always surrounded by farms, where farmers care for their vineyards and fruit orchards.

In most villages, traditional, one-story stone huts surround a public square. Under Soviet rule, many of these villages have become **collectives**, where all land and property is shared by the villagers. In a modern collective, the square is occupied by public administration buildings, where government officials determine how the **state farms** are to be run, what crops should be planted, and what tasks each farmer should be assigned. This is how farms in the Soviet Union are normally operated.

As Armenia has become more industrialized, the borders between village and city have often been obscured. Over the past fifty years or so, many villages and towns have merged into small cities. One place where this has happened is the city of Spitak in northern Armenia.

Spitak lies in the craggy range of peaks called the Bazum Mountains. With its modern buildings set into the hill-sides, the city overlooks a multitude of tiny farming villages surrounded by fields of grain and sugar beets. In 1988, many of Spitak's thirty thousand residents worked in the city's sugar processing factories, where almost all of Armenia's sugar beet crop was turned into sugar. A growing demand for sugar led to rapid growth in Spitak.

New apartments could not be built fast enough. In 1988, many people still lived in traditional, single-story houses made of stone and timber. Most of these houses were roomy, and families lived in them quite comfortably. They often owned washing machines, refrigerators, gas stoves, televisions, and other modern appliances.

But this kind of progress had not reached all of Spitak's citizens. Many poor families still lived in primitive houses of rough-hewn stones and mud. They did not even have electricity. At night, all the family members slept around a **tonir**, or central stove, in the main room to keep warm. In Spitak, as in most Armenian cities, modernization has been occurring slowly.

About 20 miles (32 kilometers) north of Spitak in the Bazum Mountains sits the beautiful city of Stepanavan. Overlooking the breathtaking Dzoraget River Canyon, the city is surrounded by forested slopes, apple orchards, and thousands of perfectly kept family gardens.

On a typical morning in Stepanavan in December 1988, women pushed babies in strollers and held their children's hands as they crossed the wide avenues. People crowded into food markets, where they often stood in long lines waiting to buy meat and vegetables. Smartly dressed men and women stepped into outdoor cafes on their way to their offices. Many of them waited in line for the high-grade cheeses, butter, and pastries for which Stepanaven is famous.

Often among them was David Gregorian, a school teacher who frequently stopped for breakfast on his way to work at a local elementary school. Standing in line, Gregorian was reminded of the frustrations of living in Armenia. Like most Armenians, however, he took the waiting for granted.

To get meat and other foods, people sometimes stood in line for an hour or

THE STATE FARMS

Over half of the people in Armenia live and work in the city. The rest live on *state farms* or smaller village *collectives* within the state farms. By law, most land and property in the Soviet Union is owned by the state. Although some farmers in Armenia and other Soviet republics own their land privately, most live and work on state farms or collectives. The goods produced on these collective farms are the property of the state and must be shared by all.

The theory behind the Soviet economy is that all citizens work according to their ability and receive according to their needs. In a free enterprise system, such as that of the United States, people can profit from private ownership. All products, whether farmed or manufactured, are owned by the individuals or corporations who produce them. These products can be sold for profit.

together by metal hooks.

Some observers warned that these buildings were like flimsy houses of cards that would quickly collapse in an earthquake. They had been built hurriedly, often with less cement and fewer steel **reinforcement** bars than required by government regulations. These and other building materials were in short supply, so builders often cut corners wherever they could.

Most of the new apartment buildings stood between four and six stories high. Aravik Danielian, who operated a large dairy farm near the city, lived on the fifth floor of one of these new apartment buildings. It was a simple but comfortable apartment with hot running water and electricity, which was used to run a television and other household appliances.

The building had arched doorways, red tile roofs, and rows of small balconies. Compared to traditional Armenian architecture, however, it was drab and colorless. Worst of all, it looked just like all the other new apartment buildings around it. The only way to tell them apart was by reading the bright red letters along the eaves of these buildings. Each building was identified by the name of the factory where most of its residents worked.

Most buildings in Leninaken's many colleges and technical schools also lacked the traditional arches, decorative **porticos**, and colorful stone work of traditional Armenian architecture. The dormitories at the university in Leninaken were austere buildings that rose eight stories high. They were built one against another in huge diagonal rows.

more. Coffee was in such short supply that each family could purchase only a small allotment each month. To buy a dress, suit, or pair of shoes, they waited as long as a week. It sometimes took months to reach the top of the waiting list for buying a car. And getting approval to move into a new apartment took a year or more.

Throughout Armenia, the housing shortage was getting worse. In Leninaken, a city of 130,000 residents about 30 miles (48 kilometers) west of Stepanavan, city officials were solving the problem by authorizing the construction of **prefabricated** apartment buildings made of concrete blocks linked

These modern buildings contrasted sharply with the beautiful buildings that lined the wide boulevards of Leninaken's main square. Most of these were stout stone buildings about four stories high. Like almost all of Armenia's historic buildings, they were made of **basalt**, marble, granite, and pink **tufa**.

One of the most beautiful of these was the cathedral in the main square. It was called Amerapurgich, meaning "savior of all people." The cathedral was built in the 1800s to be an exact replica of an eleventh century cathedral in the ancient Armenian capital of Ani. The old cathedral had been destroyed hundreds of years ago in a devastating earthquake. Inside the new cathedral was a museum filled with precious Armenian artifacts and paintings. Music from a huge pipe organ often filled the building.

In 1920, this city was given the name Leninaken. It was named after Vladimir Lenin, the founding father of the Soviet Union. Similarly, its main square was named May Uprising Square after the event that began the Russian Revolution in 1917.

Taxicab driver Dajan Haravdian knew both the traditional and modern parts of Leninaken well. In his work he often drove past the cathedral and the city square. Yet he lived in one of the new apartment buildings with his wife and two children. Haravdian's small family shows a gradual change that has taken place in Armenian culture since the country became a part of the Soviet Union in 1920. As more and more women have entered the work force, Armenian families have been getting smaller. Also, the people today have less time to devote to the large family gatherings and holiday celebrations that have been such an important part of Armenian tradition.

ARMENIA'S ARCHITECTURE

Armenia has a long tradition of architectural excellence. The ever-present danger of earthquakes requires that all buildings be strong and sturdy and that all stone masons be superior. Between the fifth and seventh centuries, Armenian architecture enjoyed its golden age. At that time, cross-shaped cathedrals crowned with domes of stone inlay dominated the landscape.

Today, the cities of Armenia contain a variety of architectural styles. Newly constructed buildings feature the columns, sculpture, and balanced forms of the classical period. And a new style, neo-Armenian, attempts to blend the classical traditions with more modern, daring innovations like sharp angles, large windows, and balconies.

Typical of the emerging Armenian woman is Dr. Hosrovik Simonion, a doctor who works in a Leninaken hospital. She specializes in prenatal care and can usually be found in the hospital's maternity ward tending to pregnant women. Her husband is a teacher at an elementary school in the city.

Men and women now work alongside each other in factories throughout Armenia, which was almost unheard of before 1920. In Leninaken in 1988, many people worked in the city's huge textile plant, the largest in Armenia. They spun cotton and wool on huge machines that twirled and slapped in a frenzy of noise, filling the air with dust and particles of fabric. Elsewhere in the city, men and women baked bread, made wine and cognac, canned fruits and meats, and packaged vegetables to be sent to Yerevan and put on cargo planes to be shipped overseas.

New factories attracted more workers to Leninaken, creating a tremendous demand for housing. As the city became more crowded, hundreds of new Russian-style, multi-story apartment buildings were quickly built on the surrounding hills. Modern ways were not always well received, but Leninaken was clearly growing and prosperous. Still, many Armenians felt like their traditional culture was slipping away.

Three
The Earth's Fury

On Wednesday, December 7, 1988, most Armenians were probably not thinking about shortages in housing, food, clothing, and luxuries, or other frustrations of living in the Soviet Union. It was the Christmas season, a time when their thoughts turned to age-old traditions and family customs. Decorated trees stood in city squares and at the entrances to stores throughout the country.

It was a cool and breezy morning in the city of Stepanavan, where crowds of shoppers strolled through the city square. As the lunch hour approached, many people headed for the pastry shops and cafes that lined the square. Meanwhile, in Stepanavan's public schools, pupils waited restlessly for noon to arrive.

At Public School No. 2, teacher David Gregorian and his students heard a buzzing noise outside. The children would not sit still. Some covered their ears as the noise grew louder.

Gregorian thought the noise might be coming from a construction site outside. He told the children to sit in their seats and calm down. But the buzzing grew even louder, and the students would not stay seated. Gregorian realized something was terribly wrong. He went to the window of his classroom, opened it, and looked down at the street.

People in the street were also looking for the source of the buzzing. They looked in the sky for a plane. Some people tried to plug their ears. Others stopped and stood, waiting for the noise to go away. But there was no escaping the strange sound.

Then Gregorian heard a muffled rumbling, like heavy trucks passing in the street below. Yet there were no trucks. Suddenly, the school buildings began to vibrate. Terrified, Gregorian realized the noise was an earthquake shaking the city. A plume of white steam burst through the pavement of the street below and shot into the air like a geyser. Water and gas pipes underground had twisted and cracked.

Gregorian turned to his students and yelled for them to stand up and follow him. He led them out of the classroom, down a stairway which was creaking and swinging back and forth, out the front door of the school, and into the street. The ground continued to shake. Cracks formed in the cement walls of the building.

Gregorian instructed the children to run across the street. Suddenly, the whole school building buckled and leaned to one side. The building's wooden beams split like twigs. Electrical wires running to the building snapped. Cement fragments shot in all directions as the structure disappeared in a huge cloud of dust.

In terror, the children ran in every direction. As Gregorian turned away from the falling debris, he saw the skyline of Stepanavan vanish behind a massive cloud of rising dust.

Twenty miles (32 kilometers) away in Spitak, the earth was shaking so violently it knocked people to the ground. Some ran for cover, while others fled from their homes. Mothers grabbed their small children and ran into the streets screaming. Buildings made of concrete and stone creaked and started **listing** to one side. Automobiles screeched to a halt in the streets as drivers lost control of their vehicles. Some drivers leapt from their cars and started to run toward the middle of the street.

A nine-story building facing the central square collapsed near its base. First it tilted over, then it folded like an accordion. A massive cloud of dust enveloped the central square, blinding those in the street. Enormous concrete slabs flew through the air, knocking over trees, park benches, and road signs. The slabs crushed pedestrians who could not move out of the way fast enough. As the slabs hit the street, they shattered into thousands of sharp fragments that flew in all directions. Screams of agony rang out everywhere.

Because they were located closest to the earthquake's **epicenter**, or origin, people in Spitak and Stepanavan were the first to feel the earthquake's destructive force. However, as the shaking of the earth radiated outward from the earthquake's epicenter, it headed down the mountain toward the villages in the Pambak Valley.

There, on the state farms, houses started to collapse. Stones, clay bricks, and glass flew as rooftops caved in. Plumes of heavy dust puffed up from each fallen home. Many of the women, young children, and other family members who were not at work were killed instantly in their collapsing houses. Others were trapped alive, pinned down by splintered beams of wood and toppled furniture. Farm buildings came crashing down on top of corrals, chicken coops, and farm machinery.

In the farm villages, hastily constructed public buildings broke apart. Shattering windows sent a rain of glass into the streets. Village after village was demolished as the seconds clicked by. Near Spitak alone, over ninety villages were flattened. The average population

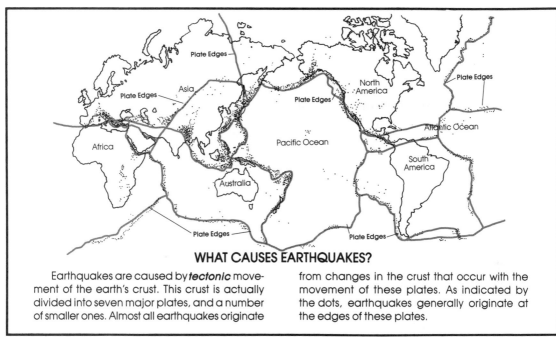

WHAT CAUSES EARTHQUAKES?

Earthquakes are caused by *tectonic* movement of the earth's crust. This crust is actually divided into seven major plates, and a number of smaller ones. Almost all earthquakes originate from changes in the crust that occur with the movement of these plates. As indicated by the dots, earthquakes generally originate at the edges of these plates.

of each of these villages was about fourteen hundred people. And in most of them, the earthquake left fewer than five hundred alive.

In the city of Leninaken, 35 miles (56.25 kilometers) south of Spitak, pedestrians in May Uprising Square were walking past the fountain that spouted a stream of water 50 feet (15 meters) into the air. But as the great iron hands of the clock tower in Leninaken's central square pointed to 11:40 A.M., the ground began to shake. The earthquake had arrived.

The fountain fell silent as underground water pipes snapped. Lenin's huge stone statue began to sway. Parents yelled to their children, who were at play in the grassy areas of the square. Ten seconds passed. At first the sidewalks and streets lurched back and forth. Then they started to move up and down. People in the square lost their balance and fell.

Someone screamed, "My God!" and pointed at the Amerapurgich Cathedral facing the square. A huge crack opened right down the middle of this great Armenian landmark, splitting it in half. Inside the church, blocks of concrete fell from the ceiling and slammed down onto the great pipe organ. The display cases filled with irreplaceable works of art and other treasures of Armenian history shattered as one of the church's walls cracked, bent over, and fell.

Many students at the city's Polytechnic Institute were walking up and down staircases to get to their next class. Almost instantly after the earthquake started, most of the staircases fell, sending screaming students to their death. Elsewhere in the city, schoolhouses swayed, creaked, and threatened to collapse. Frantically, teachers gathered their pupils and ushered them outside into playgrounds. But many did not make it before the school buildings fell.

For the next sixty seconds the earth continued to shake. Apartment complexes, which housed mostly elderly adults, women, and small children during the working hours, began to rattle violently and break apart. Windows blew out, raining shards of glass on the people running below. Walls of brick and concrete crumbled, bringing ceilings and roofs down on those trapped inside. Mothers watched helplessly as their children were crushed beneath falling bricks, beams, and slabs of concrete.

Dairy worker Aravik Danielian had milked his cows earlier in the morning and had come home to watch television. When the shaking started, his paintings fell off the walls. He thought a bomb had exploded outside. He jumped up and went to his window. Just then the television went dead as power lines coming into Leninaken were severed by falling poles.

Danielian peered out his window across the street. Buildings were crumbling and falling like dominoes. For a split second, he considered jumping out his window to escape certain death if his own building fell. He looked down to the street below. His apartment was on the fifth floor. It was too far to jump.

He ran to his front door and stood beneath the door frame. At that moment, his building collapsed, sending him straight down as though he were inside a free-falling elevator. When he landed 50 feet (15 meters) below he blacked out. But he was still alive.

Unfortunately, most people caught in collapsing apartment buildings did not get to a doorway. More than one hundred apartment buildings in Leninaken fell during the first minute of the quake.

Even before the apartments gave way, most of the city's small houses of mud and rock were destroyed, trapping their inhabitants inside. Each building that fell created its own cloud of thick dust. Within a few seconds, the wide avenues of Leninaken were completely engulfed in darkness. An immense brown cloud rose like a mushroom, as if a nuclear bomb had been detonated in the city.

In the streets, thousands of people ran for cover. Many were bleeding from cuts they had received from falling glass, and everyone choked on the dusty air. In the sudden darkness, with buildings around them in ruins, people were lost in the very streets where they had lived and worked for years.

As the dust began to settle, people looked about in shock at the piles of broken cement, bricks, iron girders, splintered wood, and glass from shattered windows. Power lines were down in the streets. Steam continued to shoot up from the ground where underground pipes had broken. People covered their eyes against the dust and tried to make their way through debris that lay in the streets and on the sidewalks. They searched frantically for others who had stood beside them only moments earlier. People yelled out names and ran into collapsed buildings looking for lost friends and family.

Four chaotic minutes passed. Then suddenly the earth began to shake again. It did not shake as hard this time, but a number of buildings that had already been badly weakened toppled down almost instantly.

SHOCK AFTER SHOCK

When two plates of the earth's crust scrape or collide, it usually causes a series of vibrations along fault lines. The vibrations may go on for days, weeks, or even months. Scientists often record these vibrations with an instrument known as a *seismograph*, and their strength is usually measured according to the *Richter scale*. The strongest of the vibrations in a series is identified as the earthquake. Weaker ones that come before it are called *foreshocks*, and weaker ones that follow the earthquake are known as *aftershocks*.

The Richter scale permits scientists to use simple numbers to compare earthquakes of an incredible range of intensities. That is because every whole number on the scale indicates a tenfold increase in strength. For example, an earthquake measuring 2.0 on the Richter scale would be 10 times stronger than a quake that measured 1.0. An earthquake measuring 3.0 would be 100 times stronger than a quake measuring 1.0, and an earthquake measured at 4.0 would be 1,000 times stronger. An earthquake measuring 7.0, roughly the measurement of the Armenian earthquake, would be 1,000,000 times stronger than a quake that measured 1.0.

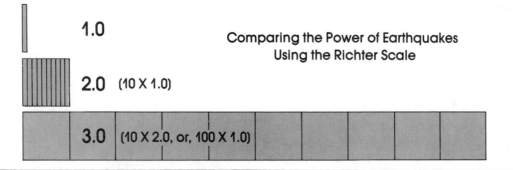

1.0

2.0 (10 X 1.0)

3.0 (10 X 2.0, or, 100 X 1.0)

Comparing the Power of Earthquakes Using the Richter Scale

32

Within five minutes of the first **aftershock** in Leninaken, fires broke out throughout the city. Most of the fires were started by broken gas pipes. Heating fuel leaked from these pipes and caught fire in the basements of numerous buildings. The buildings quickly filled with smoke and flames. People trapped inside soon died of **smoke inhalation**.

Smoke also billowed from piles of rubble where buildings once stood. Once they were ignited, fires spread quickly. Electric wires, wooden posts and beams, and other flammable material lying on the ground soon caught fire. The odor of burning corpses mingled with the smell of smoke. The fires burned out of control because most fire stations had been destroyed and many of the fire fighters killed or injured. No one was available to rescue those trapped in the burning buildings.

Every hour until nightfall, aftershocks continued to strike. Each time, survivors shuddered at the thought that another big quake might be striking.

More than half of Leninaken's build-

TRIGGERING AN EARTHQUAKE

The constant pressure and movement of the earth's plates cause earthquakes. The places on these plates where the earthquakes begin are *faults*, or cracks beneath the earth's surface. The cracks are created by the colliding plates. It is the movement of masses of rock along a fault that actually starts an earthquake.

ings, small and large alike, lay in ruins. Almost every apartment building constructed of prefabricated concrete block walls was reduced to a 40-foot-high (12-meter) mountain of rubble. Shreds of clothing, draperies, and bedding hung from concrete blocks and steel beams in mound after mound of debris.

In May Uprising Square, public buildings that had been designed in the traditional Armenian style still stood, but barely. Their stone archways were cracked and sagged precariously. Inside the buildings, some of the floors had collapsed, killing hundreds of office workers. Near the square, only the front door and altar of the beautiful Amerapurgich Cathedral still stood.

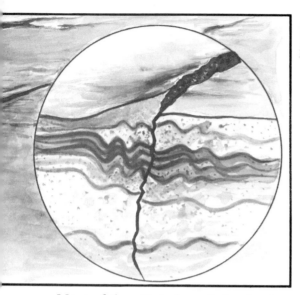

Most of the city's hospitals also lay in ruins. Near downtown Leninaken, Dr. Hosrovik Simonian had been in the maternity ward of a four-story hospital building attending to infants when the earthquake hit. Almost immediately, the upper floors of the building caved in, killing most of the doctors, nurses, and babies in the maternity ward. Dr. Simonian was still alive, but her whole body, except for her head, was pinned under three huge chunks of concrete. Fearing for her life, she began to shout for help.

For six hours, she shouted desper-ately. When she had almost lost her voice, and her hope, she heard the sound of people working to remove the pile of concrete above her. The first hand to reach her was that of her husband, who had been digging feverishly in the rubble for hours.

When the tremors from the final aftershock passed, a sudden silence spread through the towns and cities hit by the quake. In Leninaken, the great iron hands on the clock tower were frozen at 11:41. No vehicles drove on the streets. No neon signs flickered. No plume of water spouted from the foun-tain in Leninaken's central square. The only sounds that could be heard were an occasional siren in the distance, the rumbling of toppling walls, and the sobbing of grief-stricken survivors.

People pulled themselves from smashed automobiles and crawled from the wreckage of collapsed buildings. Survivors, some with cuts and bruises, others with broken arms and legs, wandered through the streets in a state of shock or utter disbelief. Cries of help rose hauntingly from beneath the rubble.

Men and women who had survived the quake at their offices, factories, and other workplaces scrambled through the rubble to get to their homes. Often they found only heaps of rock, cement, and broken boards littered with their possessions. Terrified, they searched through the crowds of stunned survivors for their families. Some were lucky and found their families quickly. Others searched frantically in the piles of rubble and listened for the cries of missing husbands, wives, and children.

Aravik Danielian, the dairy worker who had fallen five stories in his apartment building, was still alive but buried in the rubble. He had awakened a few moments after his fall and found that he was trapped beneath a massive concrete block weighing two tons. It was pitch dark and so cramped that he could barely move. His throat was parched from hours without water, yet he mus-

tered a high-pitched cry in hopes that rescuers above might hear him. His throat stung. He did not think the rescuers would reach him before he froze to death or died of thirst. Danielian did not realize that his father had begun searching for him thirty minutes after the quake. It took his father and seven other people three hours to free him.

Most people buried in the rubble, however, were not as lucky. As the afternoon passed, the full horror of the disaster began to sink in. Bodies were piled in rows at the edge of the wrecked homes, factories, and office buildings from which they had been uncovered. After running

home from work, fathers broke into tears as they recognized the bodies of their wives and children. The faces of the dead were covered with pieces of clothing found in the rubble. Men, women, and children stood crying and hugging each other.

An Armenian man wept in the street. He said:

I left my home ten minutes before it happened. I came straight back and found my wife and mother dead.

Emile Kirakosyan, the mayor of Leninaken, lost fifteen of his family members. His voice cracking with emotion, Kirakosyan cried:

I have no home or family. My wife, grandsons, everyone . . . they're all gone.

The destruction and death toll were worst within about 30 miles (48.3 kilometers) of the epicenter. Within that radius, including the cities of Spitak and Stepanavan, not one building over two stories high remained standing. Of the seven hundred thousand people who lived in this area, only two hundred thousand still had homes.

Sixty-five miles (104.5 kilometers) from the epicenter, in the capital city of Yerevan, buildings shook hard but none fell. To the north, in Soviet Georgia, about 70 miles (113 kilometers) from the epicenter, only a few buildings were damaged. More than 200 miles away (322 kilometers) from the epicenter, in Turkey, Iran, and the Soviet Union, people felt the quake's tremors, but no damage occurred.

As the night of December 7, 1988, wore on, many of the roughly five hundred thousand people left homeless by the quake gathered in the public parks and city squares of the most heavily damaged region of Armenia. They had no food and hardly any warm clothing. Yet they had to wait through the night and the following day before help arrived. And every hour that passed, approximately another four hundred Armenians trapped in the rubble died.

Courtesy of Rev. Berdj Djambazian

Four
Buried Alive

The next morning the smoke that rose from thousands of campfires gave the sky above Spitak a blood-red hue. Survivors, still smeared with blood and tears, sat speechless on park benches or crouched in the ruins of homes or other buildings. Using shreds of cloth and whatever else they could find, people tended the wounds of loved ones, friends, and even strangers. Some still slept near the smoldering coals of their campfires. Others stood at the fires wrapped in coats, layers of clothing, strips of carpet, and anything they could salvage to keep them warm.

Corpses lay everywhere in the destroyed cities, twisted and contorted in death, many smeared with blood and covered in a thick coating of brown dust. Some survivors began to enter destroyed buildings and drag out the dead. They placed bodies carefully in rows in front of the collapsed factories, offices, schools, and homes.

Others searched through these rows for missing family members. Survivors trudged all over the city to identify their loved ones and take them away, some carrying away tiny babies who had been killed in the disaster. Many people buried their own family members without priests or proper funerals. Trenches were dug in the snowy terrain outside Leninaken. Coffins were placed in the trenches, end to end, like long trains of miniature boxcars.

Since so many police officers had been killed in the quake, no organized police force was on duty. Looters took advantage of this and stole from unprotected shops, offices, and banks. Other looters preyed on the corpses that could be found in every collapsed building. They stripped them of their clothes, wristwatches, necklaces, rings, and even the gold in their teeth.

In Spitak, all but a handful of the residents had lost everything. Whole families, suddenly without homes, huddled together and wept. Many people, not lucky enough to have found family members alive, sat trembling in the cold alone. Children roamed the streets unaware that their parents lay dead in the rubble.

For most survivors, there was little to do but wait for help. They figured that they would soon be evacuated from the destroyed cities. In these cities, there was no electricity, no running water, no ambulances, fire trucks, or other emergency vehicles to rescue those trapped beneath the rubble. Patiently, the people of Spitak waited.

But for the thousands of people buried alive, time was running out. Many were bleeding, others suffered from traumatic shock. Slowly, another full day passed and the bitter cold of another night fell upon Armenia.

It was forty-eight hours after the quake before people in the capital city of Yerevan heard the sound of jetliners overhead. Airplanes loaded with supplies and volunteers—called mercy flights—roared into Yerevan International Airport. Other planes soon started arriving at Leninaken Airport. The first planes came from Soviet Georgia. Soon planes from France, West Germany, Italy, and Cuba arrived, all bringing food, medical supplies, and rescue equipment.

For two full days, the Armenians had waited for this outside help to arrive. Then, all at once, help arrived from so many directions that confusion reigned. No one was in charge of coordinating the rescue effort.

At the Leninaken Airport, airplanes parked to unload their cargo in the middle of the airfield, blocking the way for other airplanes to land. There were not enough people nor enough equipment to unload all the planes. Even with the help of volunteers, it took hours to unload each plane. Meanwhile, the sky filled with arriving planes that had to circle the airport waiting for a chance to land.

As more planes arrived, the problem grew worse. A plane carrying a team of British fire fighters and doctors landed. It carried a number of heat-sensing devices used to find people buried in the rubble. Thirty-seven rescuers with search dogs and supplies flew in from Switzerland; then dozens of medical specialists came from India. Next, ten planes swooped in carrying supplies from the United States government, followed by twelve planes filled with food and supplies sent by American corporations. Before long, more than three hundred planeloads of heavy equipment, supplies, and clothing had arrived from forty-six countries.

By Friday, December 9, it had started to rain. The road coming into Leninaken turned into a muddy path. It was jammed with a caravan of emergency supply trucks, ambulances, and automobiles trying to enter the city to help earthquake victims. Cars and trucks were loaded with bread, blankets, and pillows. Some came loaded with black wooden boxes—homemade coffins in which to bury the dead. Alongside the road, hundreds of people from the villages trudged through the mud into the demolished cities in search of family members and relatives. They passed thousands of survivors who were leaving the destroyed city on foot. Having lost everything they owned, many decided to leave the city and go to live with friends or relatives in other parts of Armenia.

Traffic was also jammed on the only road into Spitak. The earthquake had split the road down the middle, and in places, the gap was wide enough to swallow a bulldozer. The road was built directly over a fault line, and the crack followed the narrow road through Spitak and up to the mountains. Before equipment could be brought into the city, the crack had to be filled with sand.

As the hours passed, more trapped people died from injuries, from lack of water, or from shock. Survivors made courageous attempts to rescue as many of the buried as they could. Groups of men clambered through the rubble and clawed at heaps of concrete and steel with their bare hands. They had few shovels and no earth-moving equipment. At night, they worked by the light of campfires. Many choked back tears as they dug. They, too, had lost loved ones in the disaster.

Lernik Yeremyan, a medical student in Leninaken, took command of a group of Armenians trying to rescue people. His team worked all day and all night uncovering the buried. Yeremyan recalls the frustrations that they encountered:

At the beginning [of the rescue] there was nothing. No cranes. No cutting gear. No lights. Nothing. Our rescue team was just sixty people standing around and yelling at each other.

By late Friday, two days after the earthquake, rescue teams finally entered the destroyed cities. They went to work immediately, joining survivors who were already sifting through the rubble in search of people still alive. They scrambled gingerly atop ruined buildings, listening for the cries of people. They set up electronic sensing devices and listened for the breathing of those buried and unconscious.

When they found people trapped in the rubble, they cleared away the debris above them, then lifted them carefully onto stretchers and carried them to temporary first-aid stations throughout the city.

Many victims needed medical help. However, medical supply shortages and delays made it difficult to save many of the trapped. These shortages also made it less likely that victims pulled from the rubble would survive.

Rescue efforts were still hampered by disorganization. As a result, rescue attempts were haphazard. When trained search dogs in one area found a victim trapped in the rubble, crane operators and communication equipment often sat idle in another area.

Tragically, the same kind of chaos prevailed in the skies above the Yerevan and Leninaken airports. A Soviet military transport plane, bringing in Soviet soldiers to help rescue victims, got lost in the fog, veered off course, and slammed into the airport in Leninaken, killing all seventy-nine people aboard. Another air disaster followed the next day when a Yugoslavian air force transport plane collided with another plane near the congested airport in Yerevan, killing its crew of seven.

As more days passed, the temperature dropped and snow fell. Soon, Spitak lived up to its name, which means "all white." Buildings leaning to one side and heaps of rubble now looked like snow-laden foothills and cliffs. The snow and the cold made the rescue work even slower. Undaunted, rescuers worked on.

In Spitak, a crane lifted a huge concrete slab. Then workers dug and chipped away for hours to remove three bodies from the rubble. Nearby, a young man watched in horror as he saw the frozen bodies of his mother, wife, and child, his child still in its mother's arms, lifted from the ruins.

Yet amid the misery there were miracles. Dajan Haravdian, the Leninaken taxi driver, had gone with his fifteen-year-old son to help dig out survivors. "We kept hearing faint cries for help,"

A DELICATE BALANCE

Rescuing victims trapped beneath collapsed buildings is both delicate and dangerous work. After an earthquake, concrete, wood, and other building materials lie on the ground in unstable piles. Walking too quickly through these piles, stepping in the wrong spot, or removing the wrong piece of material may cause the whole pile to collapse. In Armenia, a number of people died immediately after the earthquake by rushing carelessly into the piles of rubble to rescue someone.

Trained rescue teams use stethoscopes, heat-seeking cameras, infra-red detectors, and trained search dogs to locate trapped victims. When they find someone, expert rescuers usually work their way toward the victim from the side of a pile, rather than from the top. To have a chance at success, they must work slowly and carefully. Cranes, jackhammers, and other heavy equipment are of little help. Instead, the small picks and axes used by mountain climbers are the best tools for an earthquake rescue operation.

he remembers. "But how much could we do with bare hands?"

One time, however, as they cleared away chunks of concrete, they came upon a deep hole in the ruins. Suddenly, two hands appeared out of the darkness pushing a bundle toward Haravdian and his son. The bundle was a two-month-old baby girl, who was still alive. Haravdian and his son helped the child and her father from the hole. Haravdian recognized the man as the clock maker from across the street. They had been under the rubble, waiting to be found, for two days.

An even more incredible event followed. When a large sixteen-ton crane finally arrived in Leninaken from Yerevan, it was used to lift a large concrete slab covering a factory basement. When the slab was pulled away, two hundred workers emerged, hungry and bewildered, but otherwise unharmed.

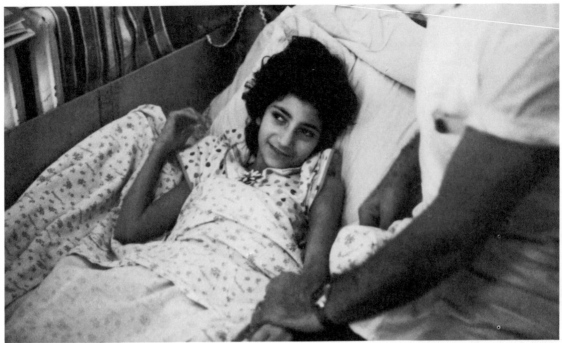

After four days, over fifteen thousand people had been rescued alive from the rubble. But many of these died because makeshift hospitals ran out of medical supplies. Some survivors were placed on planes and trucks and taken to hospitals in Yerevan. The hospitals there were soon so crowded that doctors released other patients to make room for the victims.

Inside the crowded operating rooms, children with broken limbs, bruised bodies, and bandaged heads lay two or three to a bed. Hardly comprehending what had happened, some of them called out, "Mother!" or "Father!" Unfortunately, few parents were present to answer their calls.

With every passing day, rescuers found fewer and fewer people alive in the rubble. Seven days after the quake, the cries from beneath the rubble had faded. One rescue worker said:

Until yesterday we could still hear voices. Now nothing.

On December 17, ten days after the earthquake, Soviet officials announced that the cities of Spitak and Leninaken would be cleared by bulldozers. But the citizens in these cities protested that many missing people were still unaccounted for. They refused to abandon their demolished neighborhoods.

Although trucks with loudspeakers cruised through the streets, and soldiers pleaded with citizens to leave, thousands of Armenians continued their vigil. They set up camps next to their crumpled houses and kept a twenty-four-hour watch for bulldozers. That day twenty-one people were found alive, and the Soviets agreed to halt the bulldozers for a few more days. Four more people were rescued on December 18, and one on December 19. On December 20, Artur Arutunian was pulled from the rubble in Leninaken after being buried in the dark for thirteen days. He was the last survivor to be rescued from the Armenian earthquake.

On December 21, fourteen days after the quake, the rescue was officially called off when Soviet authorities decided that no more survivors were likely to be found. A Soviet official announced:

> There are [no more people] to be found. I think everybody knows that by now.

The two thousand foreign rescuers abandoned their search. Although thousands of victims had been rescued, at least twenty-five thousand others had died. Some Armenians believe that thousands more could have been saved if rescuers had been better organized and responded more quickly to the crisis. They blame Soviet authorities for not coordinating the rescue effort more effectively. In one case, for example, a relief team refused to deliver food to starving villagers because all of the government officials in the village had been killed. The officials were the only ones authorized to accept the shipment. Other workers refused to allow people to bury their dead family members before the proper paperwork had been filled out.

Much of the frustration, resentment, and distrust of the Soviet government continued to build. In some ways the disaster relief efforts had made things worse, and the Armenians did not know who to blame.

Five
Political Aftershocks

On December 8, 1988, the day after the earthquake, as survivors wandered the crumpled, debris-littered streets in shock, a press helicopter landed in Spitak. Out of the dust whipped up by the helicopter's propellers stepped NBC Nightly News anchorman Tom Brokaw. Mr. Brokaw and his camera team made their way to the ruins of the massive Spitak bread factory, where they broadcast a news report to America. This was the first time that any American news report about a disaster had been broadcast live from the Soviet Union. In fact, this was the first time in the twentieth century that Western journalists were free to investigate and report on a disaster inside the Soviet Union.

Previously, the movements of foreign reporters had been closely monitored and their reports carefully censored. Following Brokaw's lead, a stampede of reporters from around the world descended on the destroyed cities and began wiring dramatic stories back home about the earthquake rescue effort.

The press reported that the entire Soviet nation was mobilized to help the Armenian people. They were told that even the neighboring Soviet republic of Azerbaijan, though embroiled in a violent land dispute with Armenia, sent truckloads of volunteers and supplies. The Azerbaijanis had set their political interests aside and come to the aid of their arch enemies, the Armenians. So too, Turkey, a longtime enemy of Armenia, came to the aid of the earthquake victims. It sent a convoy of trucks bearing medical supplies, blood transfusion equipment, and food.

Although these reports were true, some reporters wondered if they were getting the full picture of Armenia in crisis. One American reporter concluded:

The Soviets have orchestrated the press coverage to convey an uplifting, but exaggerated, image of a country united in its tragedy.

The president of the Soviet Union, Mikhail Gorbachev, did his best to convey this unity and gain worldwide support for the Armenians.

The Soviet foreign ministry escorted reporters on tours and organized helicopter flyovers. Journalists were permitted to hire private cars or hitchhike rides on rescue trucks. This was all part of the government's new policy of openness, or *glasnost*. As a result, most reports gave a favorable impression of the Soviet government and people, unified in their efforts to aid the Armenians.

When the earthquake struck, Gorbachev was delivering an important speech at the United Nations in New York City. Later that night, Gorbachev's staff informed him of the terrible events occurring in Armenia. Immediately, he decided to cut his trip to the United States short.

The next morning, he arrived at Kennedy International Airport in New York. Gorbachev emerged from a black limousine, then stepped up to a podium to make a statement to the American people. Many Americans had been deeply moved by news of the earthquake.

"I would like to thank the American people," Mikhail Gorbachev told the crowd, "for their feelings of sympathy and for their readiness to give assistance in this difficult hour. Goodbye," he said sadly. "Thank you."

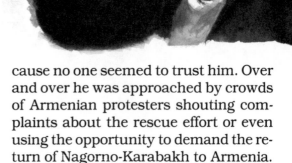

When Mikhail and Raisa Gorbachev landed in Moscow, they were greeted by hundreds of Armenian protesters carrying banners and chanting grievances in the streets. And when they arrived in Armenia, most of the people there did not welcome them with open arms. Instead, they were jeered and whistled at. Many people spat on the ground in disgust. With photographers snapping photos and TV cameras whirring, Gorbachev listened to the Armenians' complaints.

One man asked angrily, "Why hadn't officials in Moscow predicted the earthquake?" Another shouted, "Why had the rescue effort been so slow, causing many people to die needlessly?"

At each stop he made in Armenia, Gorbachev was received in the same way. He was shocked and angered be-cause no one seemed to trust him. Over and over he was approached by crowds of Armenian protesters shouting complaints about the rescue effort or even using the opportunity to demand the return of Nagorno-Karabakh to Armenia.

Distrust prompted others to ask whether Armenian children who had lost their parents in the quake would be sent north, into Russia, and never returned to their homeland. This fear stems from the memory of the 1915 Armenian genocide.

Gorbachev was stunned by the questions and he responded angrily:

The things they say! They think we want to take the children away to Russia and not return them to Armenia, to tear them away from their people. Do they think we are going to deport the Armenians to Siberia?

Soon, events turned even uglier. The Soviet press printed editorials claiming that the relief effort had been hampered by a group of well-known Armenian nationalists who had spread rumors about Soviet mistreatment of Armenians. The newspapers said this had prompted the protests across Armenia. Following the appearance of these editorials, Soviet security police arrested five prominent Armenian nationalists in Yerevan. The police officials claimed that the nationalists had tried to take control of the Armenian republic after the earthquake. Few Armenians believed them, however, and rumors spread quickly that Gorbachev had ordered the arrests.

Many Armenians began to suspect Gorbachev of using the earthquake tragedy as an excuse to clamp down on the Armenian protest movement. They claimed that the arrests had taken place immediately after the earthquake so that no one would notice. Some people picketed in the streets, demanding the release of the political activists.

In Yerevan, demonstrations became violent and angry protesters set fires in the streets and clashed with Soviet troops. Many of the rioters were arrested and given thirty-day jail sentences for causing disorder. One Soviet official said that Gorbachev had gone to the United States to talk about peace, but when he returned, it was "like coming into a war."

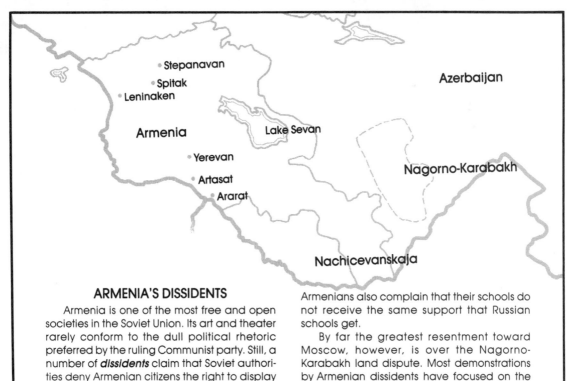

ARMENIA'S DISSIDENTS

Armenia is one of the most free and open societies in the Soviet Union. Its art and theater rarely conform to the dull political rhetoric preferred by the ruling Communist party. Still, a number of *dissidents* claim that Soviet authorities deny Armenian citizens the right to display their national pride. Armenians are forced to use Russian as their official language. Some

Armenians also complain that their schools do not receive the same support that Russian schools get.

By far the greatest resentment toward Moscow, however, is over the Nagorno-Karabakh land dispute. Most demonstrations by Armenian dissidents have focused on the demand that this strip of land, now controlled by Azerbaijan, be returned to Armenia.

On December 11, while rescue planes were still arriving, Soviet troops also arrived in Yerevan to dispel the mounting violence and unrest. The following morning, December 12, the Soviet press carried articles begging people to "first be human beings, then ...Armenians or Azerbaijanis." But clearly, whatever momentary unity had existed between the two peoples because of the earthquake had disappeared.

On December 22, 1988, the last rescue teams left Armenia. As their airplanes disappeared into the gray hori-zon, snow covered most of the country. The temperature hovered steadily at 10 degrees below zero Fahrenheit (23.5 degrees below zero Celsius). Weary rescue volunteers peered from their airplane windows down onto the ruins of the city where they had worked to save lives.

Armenia was devastated: 380 schools and universities lost, along with 84 hospitals, 86 million square feet (26 million square meters) of housing, 58 villages, 90 collectives, and 209 state farms. The death toll had risen above 25,000.

As survivors lay in their hospital beds, the physical wounds began to heal, but psychological wounds began to set in. The average survivor had lost between ten and fifteen relatives in the earthquake, and many had lost all of their possessions.

A month after the disaster, tent cities were spread over the vacant areas of Stepanavan, Spitak, and Leninaken to house some of the 520,000 people that the quake had left homeless. Almost every school in these cities had been destroyed, so children played in the desolate streets. Most orphaned children had been taken to existing or temporary orphanages. One temporary orphanage was created in a resort hotel on the mountain slopes above crystal blue Lake Sevan.

Other orphaned children were taken in by relatives or friends. On a street in Spitak, one orphaned child was held in his aunt's arms. The woman bit the edge of her shawl while looking nervously at the devastated buildings around her. Pointing to a now-flattened city block where a crane was hoisting a giant boulder, she cried, "Look, that was the sugar factory!"

She pointed across the street. "That was the bread factory! And next to it, the kindergarten!"

Children's school desks lay strewn in the mud, still decorated with the children's drawings.

"What has happened to us?" she screamed.

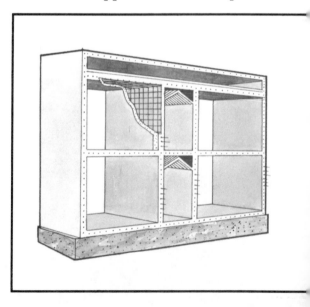

Collision Zone

Fault

Six
What Happened, and Why

Following the worst natural disaster in Armenian history, many Armenians, like the woman in Spitak, were bewildered. They did not understand why such a devastating earthquake had struck this heavily populated region of Armenia. More importantly, many people wondered if the cities and villages in this area could have been better prepared for the earthquake.

Even before the quake, geologists were well aware of the fault lines running beneath the cities of Spitak, Stepanavan, and Leninaken. Could buildings in these cities have been built to withstand the effects of an earthquake? Could rescue efforts have been better organized to help quake victims? Soon after the quake, geologists, architects, engineers, and government officials converged on these cities to find some answers.

In an earthquake, the actual shaking of the earth does not kill anyone. Rather, people are killed when buildings collapse or catch on fire. Among the first buildings to fall in the Armenian earthquake were those that rested on columns instead of solid foundations. Architects call this kind of foundation soft support.

Many large buildings erected on solid foundations, especially those that did not stand too close together, remained standing. They may have swayed drastically, their roofs may have

caved in, and they might have sustained serious damage, but after the shaking stopped, their walls were still standing.

Other buildings could have withstood the earthquake, but they were built too close together. During the quake they swayed so much that the tops of the buildings crashed together, causing at least the upper floors to collapse.

Lithosphere

Fault

Asthenosphere

Even buildings that did not appear damaged from the outside were often badly damaged inside. Ceilings, lighting fixtures, bookshelves, and banks of computers came crashing down, often crushing people who stood below them. Fires broke out when boilers, generators, and gas pipes broke. Then buildings quickly filled with smoke and flames,

EARTHQUAKE-RESISTANT BUILDINGS

Armenian architects and engineers are designing new buildings for the destroyed cities, buildings that can withstand a major earthquake. Solid concrete foundations are a good start. Central concrete columns inside tall apartment and office buildings will strengthen them. In case a building does collapse in an earthquake, ceilings suspended below each concrete floor will help shield the people inside.

No matter how well-designed they are, these new buildings must be constructed better than those that collapsed in the earthquake. There can be no skimping on building materials. Concrete walls must be reinforced with plenty of steel rods, and mortar must contain enough cement for maximum strength.

killing most of the people trapped inside.

After the disaster, hundreds of foreign scientists, engineers, and architects visited Armenia. They found that Soviet *seismologists* had underestimated the potential intensity of earthquakes in this region. Most buildings were designed to withstand an earthquake measuring 6.0 or less on the *Richter scale*. The quake that hit Armenia on December 7, 1988, measured 6.9, approximately nine times more powerful than a 6.0 quake.

But the *magnitude* of the earthquake does not tell the whole story. The destructive power of a quake comes from a combination of the intensity and the direction of the earth's vibrations. A *seismograph* measures the intensity of vibrations, but not the direction. If the ground vibrates both horizontally and vertically during an earthquake, the destructive power is much greater than if the stress is all in the same direction. In the Armenian earthquake, the earth shook in both directions at once.

Another reason for the tremendous destruction was the poor construction quality of many of Armenia's buildings. But it was not easy to determine why these buildings had been so poorly built. City planners required that all buildings be designed to withstand earthquakes. They also required official inspections of construction sites to make sure that the design specifications were being met.

Most observers concluded that these inspections must not have been very thorough, if they took place at all. In some cases, inspection requirements conflicted with other government requirements. For example, builders were required to complete a certain number of new buildings each year. Since supplies of cement and steel reinforcement bars were scarce, many builders took shortcuts wherever possible.

They put fewer steel bars into concrete walls than required. They mixed their concrete with more sand and less cement than required. And they sealed the joints between concrete blocks with mud instead of mortar. As evidence was gathered, it became increasingly clear that no single group could be blamed for the poor earthquake preparation. But it also became clear that many buildings were not even sturdy enough to withstand a 6.0 earthquake, let alone a much stronger one.

Placing blame was not as important to the Armenians as rebuilding the destroyed cities and villages so that they could better withstand the next earthquake. The first step however was cleaning up the rubble and ruins. Demolition teams used dynamite to demolish the remains of buildings. Even dynamite was in short supply, however, so the demolition went slowly.

Huge Soviet army tanks, along with tanks from Italy, Belgium, and Germany, rattled through the streets,

giving Spitak the appearance of a city at war. The tanks pushed down weakened buildings that still stood. They towed tall cranes, which were used to pull down roofs and balconies. Dump trucks hauled debris to the outskirts of the city, where it was burned.

When the cleanup was finished, a massive rebuilding plan had to be put into action. Hospitals were needed immediately to treat the seventeen thousand people who had been injured in the earthquake. The country had also lost 130 factories. New ones were needed, not only to provide essential goods, but also jobs for the 170,000 people who had been left jobless. New schools had to be built, and orphanages were needed to care for the children without families.

The greatest challenge, however, would be building new housing for over five hundred thousand people whose homes had been destroyed. Nine months after the earthquake, most of these people were still living in tents outside Spitak and Leninaken. Shortages of cement, stone, windows, and plumbing materials delayed construction. And with the eyes of the world upon them, builders could not take the same old shortcuts. The country needed mining equipment, cement plants, and factories to make glass, pipe, and electrical wire. Also, government officials realized that new apartments would be of no use if there were no factories nearby to provide jobs. Similarly, new schools would have to be built for the families that moved into the new apartments.

Though these needs had to be met quickly, architects and builders could not repeat the mistakes of the past. Stable buildings had to be constructed so that this disaster would not be repeated. All new structures had to conform to stricter building codes. A law was passed shortly after the quake forbidding new buildings in earthquake-prone areas to be over four stories tall. No buildings at all could be built directly over known fault lines.

Because of these tougher codes, some villages had to be entirely relocated. These new codes also affected cities and villages that were not severely damaged by the Spitak quake. For example, many buildings in the capital, Yerevan, have been reinforced in case the next earthquake strikes closer to this city.

All this rebuilding presented the Armenian people with an enormous challenge. Planners predicted that the job would take five to ten years, if the necessary money and building materials were available. To show its commit-

OPERATION SEARCH

A *telecommunications* system called Search was set up the day after the earthquake to help survivors and Armenians living abroad locate missing family members. Over one hundred thousand names were entered into a computer data base. People living outside Armenia contacted the Search center in Yerevan by phone, radio, or telegraph. Photos of unidentified children in hospitals were published by Search in a newsletter called *Hope*. In all, Search helped unite over twenty-two thousand victims with family or friends.

ment to Armenia and to the unity of the Soviet Union, the Soviet government required each of the other fourteen Soviet republics to contribute to Armenia's rebuilding. Every republic was assigned a different region of Armenia to help rebuild.

To make the rebuilding go as smoothly as possible, the Soviet Union invited teams of architects from Norway, Italy, and the United States to join Soviet architects in designing the reconstructed cities. The American team proposed rebuilding the city of Spitak on a hillside. Their plan combined traditional Armenian architecture, including the use of tufa stone, with more modern design features.

Armenian planners were amazed when they saw this plan. The Americans seemed to have captured Armenian tradition better than the Armenian architects themselves. The plan for Spitak, the first American-designed city in the Soviet Union, was adopted.

For the first time since World War II, the Soviet Union had accepted disaster aid and assistance from Western countries. In the past, the Soviet Union had refused such assistance. In 1985, for example, after a nuclear reactor exploded in the town of Chernobyl, the Soviets refused to accept much aid from foreign countries. It was as if they wanted to prove to the world that they could handle their disasters without outside help.

Glasnost in the USSR also made it possible for Armenians living in the United States to help relatives and other disaster victims as soon as they heard about the earthquake. They were permitted to set up a **telecommunication**

network, called Search, between Soviet Armenia and the United States. The network helped Armenians in the United States get information about relatives and friends affected by the disaster.

Improved relations between the United States and the Soviet Union also made it possible for Americans to provide medical treatment to earthquake victims. In fact, eighty severely injured children were flown to American hospitals. They were the first Soviet victims to be treated in American hospitals since World War II. The effort was organized by Project Hope, an American volunteer organization.

A POTENTIAL NUCLEAR DISASTER?

Engineers have discovered that a nuclear power plant near the capital city of Yerevan is only built to withstand an earthquake of 6.5—four times less intense than the Armenian earthquake. If the *epicenter* had been 25 to 30 miles (40 to 50 kilometers) farther west, this earthquake could have damaged the power plant and caused a serious nuclear disaster.

PREDICTING EARTHQUAKES

For years, geologists have based their predictions of earthquakes on the seismic gap theory. According to this theory, powerful earthquakes usually occur along the part of a fault line where there has been little or no earthquake activity for several years. During this time, pressure caused by plates moving beneath the surface continues to build. In locations where this pressure is occasionally released through minor earthquakes, a major earthquake is less likely to occur.

The seismic gap theory helps identify a region where a major earthquake is likely. But it cannot pinpoint precisely when the quake will occur. Scientists are looking for ways to make more precise predictions. They know that shifts in the earth's crust sometimes signal a coming earthquake. So they use instruments called *tiltmeters* to detect changes in the slope of land near a fault. *Gravimeters* are used to check the *density* of the ground. If the density at a specific location changes, it means that rock beneath the surface has moved.

Space technology is also helpful for predicting earthquakes. Lasers positioned on opposite sides of a fault direct their beams to a satellite in space. The beams are reflected off the satellite back to the earth. Incredibly small changes in the angle and travel time of these laser beams can be recorded and used to pinpoint minute movements along a fault line.

Yet with all these sophisticated methods, people are not as good at recognizing the immediate signs of an earthquake as animals are. In China, where earthquakes occur frequently, scientists have observed strange animal behavior just before a violent earthquake strikes. Cows and horses refuse to enter their pens, dogs howl, birds screech, rats run around in circles, and frogs jump out of their ponds. By evacuating cities and villages whenever these animal behaviors have been observed, officials in China have saved thousands of lives.

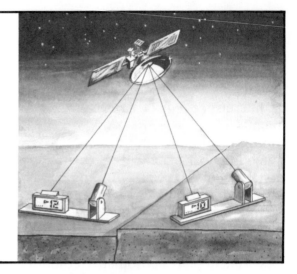

Through this and other efforts, five hundred million dollars in charity donations from 113 countries was raised in the first six months after the disaster. In Spitak, Norwegian teams erected a 250-bed hospital. The Italians constructed an entire village just outside the destroyed city, complete with a hospital, school, clinic, and children's center. Czechoslovakian engineers built a new school there for 750 children, while Finland and Italy teamed up to build a rehabilitation center for people who had suffered spinal injuries in the earthquake. In the city of Leninaken, the Cubans and the British built new schools. France erected apartment buildings, while West Germany, Poland, and Italy set up clinics to treat the injured.

The worldwide outpouring of aid, however generous, barely scratched the surface of Armenia's needs. The total damage from the earthquake was estimated at sixteen billion dollars. The cost would be difficult for the Soviet Union to bear alone. Foreign support would be a vital part of the rebuilding effort for years to come, but the greatest demand was on the Armenians themselves. They would have to show the courage and leadership needed to rebuild their cities and villages.

As they have done so many times in the past, the Armenians joined together to help each other. Even poor families helped, sharing their food, money, and clothing with the earthquake victims. Workers, organized through labor unions, opened special savings accounts to raise money for the victims. Poor and rich people from throughout Armenia traveled to the disaster area to lend a hand in the rebuilding effort.

In the weeks and months following the earthquake, images of both despair and hope clashed everywhere. In a small town stadium outside Leninaken, a young man searched for his brother in the sea of coffins that filled the stadium. He opened the lid of each coffin until he found him. Weeping uncontrollably, he climbed into the coffin and lay down beside his brother, attempting to join the dead. In one village, so many people had perished that a woman shuddered and cried out, "We have no tears left!"

But amid the misery there was hope. There was also the strong Armenian will to survive despite their long history of tragedies.

"Let me show you something," said Mordechai Goldenberg, an Israeli physician, to another visitor who had come to assist after the disaster.

He led the visitor into a special room in the hospital where he had been working. Inside, two Armenian women lay with newborn babies in their arms, both delivered in the chaotic days following the quake. Said Goldenberg:

The sight of those babies will keep us all alive for awhile.

Glossary

aftershock . . . . A minor earthquake that follows a stronger earthquake and originates from the same spot.

annex . . . . To add a region to an existing country, state, or territory.

asthenosphere . . . . [as-**THEN**-uh-sfeer] The flexible layer of the earth's crust which lies beneath the lithosphere.

basalt . . . . [buh-**SALT**] A dark, tough, fine-grained volcanic rock.

Byzantine Empire . . . . . . [**BIZ**-un-teen] An ancient empire in southeast Europe and southwest Asia centered in what is now Turkey.

collective . . . . A rural village on a state farm. The families in a collective share the profits of the farm.

Constantinople . . . . Capital city of the ancient Byzantine Empire. Now known as Istanbul.

crust . . . . The surface, or outermost layer of rock covering the earth.

density . . . . The ratio of a material's mass to its volume or size. For example, solid rock is more dense than sand.

diaspora . . . . [dye-**AS**-puh-ruh] A scattering of people who have a common nationality.

dissident . . . . One who actively expresses disagreement.

epicenter . . . . [**EP**-uh-center] The area on the earth's surface directly above the origin of an earthquake.

ethnic . . . . Having to do with a group of people who share a common language, culture, and history.

fault . . . . A crack or fracture in the earth's crust caused by the movement of tectonic plates.

foreshock . . . . A minor earthquake that preceeds a stronger earthquake and originates from the same spot.

genocide . . . . [**JEN**-uh-side] A planned program for killing all the people of a certain nationality or race.

glasnost . . . . [**GLOSS**-noast] The Soviet policy of openness in the news media.

gravimeter . . . . [gruh-**VIM**-uh-ter] An instrument used to measure density.

guerrilla . . . . Having to do with a small force of irregular or volunteer soldiers making surprise raids.

list . . . . To lean or tilt.

lithosphere . . . . [**LITH**-uh-sfeer] The rigid outer layer of the earth's crust.

Macedonia . . . . [mass-uh-**DOE**-nee-uh] An ancient kingdom of southeast Europe now divided among Greece, Yugloslavia, and Bulgaria.

magnitude . . . . Size or extent.

migrate . . . . To move from one place to another to live.

Mongols . . . . The people of the Mongol Empire, which once ruled much of Asia and eastern Europe.

nationalists . . . . Those who actively support national independence.

oppression . . . . Rule by force.

Persia . . . . An ancient empire centered in what is now Iran.

plate . . . . One of several large, moving sections of the earth's surface.

portico . . . . A porch with a roof supported by columns.

prefabricated . . . . Manufactured in sections that can be shipped and quickly assembled.

purge . . . . To remove persons considered harmful, dangerous, or disloyal.

regime . . . . [ruh-**ZHEEM**] Government.

reinforcement . . . . Added strength.

republic . . . . A state or nation in which voters elect officials.

Richter scale . . . . A scale for measuring the strength of an earthquake.

seismograph . . . . An instrument that records and measures vibrations of the earth's surface.

seismologist . . . . A scientist who studies earthquakes.

smoke inhalation . . . . The potentially fatal condition of breathing smoke into the lungs.

state farm . . . . A farm owned by the government.

tectonic . . . . Pertaining to changes in the earth's crust.

telecommunication . . . . . Electronic communication, such as radio, telephone, television, and computer.

tiltmeter . . . . An instrument for measuring angles of slope.

tonir . . . . [toe-**NEAR**] A traditional Armenian oven made of yellow stones and built into the ground.

tufa . . . . [**TOO**-fuh] A pink, porous, volcanic rock.

Further Reading

THE ARMENIAN EARTHQUAKE

"A Shattered Land," *Life*, Feb., 1989, 36.

"The Killer Quake that Shook the World." *U.S. News & World Report*, Dec. 19, 1988: 10-11.

Brand, David. "When the Earth Shook." *Time*, Dec. 19, 1988: 34-39.

Cooper, Nancy and Hurt, Harry, III. "Agony in Armenia." *Newsweek*, Dec. 19, 1988.

Wertsman, Vladimir. *The Armenians in America 1618-1976*. New York: Oceana Publications, Inc., 1978.

ARMENIA & THE USSR

Aslanyan, A.A. *Soviet Armenia*. Moscow: Progress Publishers, 1971.

Bedoukian, Kerop. *Some of Us Survived: The Story of an Armenian Boy*. New York: Farrar Straus Giroux, 1979.

Kherdian, David. *The Road From Home: The Story of an Armenian Girl*. New York: Greenwillow Books, 1979.

Killingray, David. *Stalin*. St. Paul, Minnesota: Greenhaven Press, 1980.

Louis, Victor and Louis, Jennifer. *The Complete Guide to the Soviet Union*. London: Michael Joseph's, 1976.

Lydolph, Paul E. *Geography of the U.S.S.R.* New York: John Wiley & Sons, 1970.

Malcom, Vartan M. *The Armenians in Armenia*. Boston: The Pilgrim's Press, 1919.

Nagel's Encyclopedia Guide—USSR. Geneva: Nagal Publishers, 1985.

Sayder, Louis Leo. *The First Book of the Soviet Union*. New York: Franklin Watts, 1978.

Theyer, Charles Wheeler. *Russia*. New York: Time, Inc., 1965.

EARTHQUAKES

Halacy, D.S. Jr. *Earthquakes: A Natural History*. Indianapolis and New York: The Bobbs-Merrill Co., Inc., 1974.

Iacopi, Robert. *Earthquake Country*. Menlo Park, California: Lane Publishing Co., 1971.

Walker, Bryce. *Earthquake*. Alexandria, Virginia: Time-Life Books, 1982.

Other Works Consulted

The Armenian Observer, January 25, 1989.

Foster, Robert J. *General Geology, 2d ed.* Columbus: Charles E. Merrill Publishing Co., 1969.

Hovannisian, Richard G. *Armenia: On the Road to Independence.* Berkeley and Los Angeles: University of California Press, 1967.

Hovannisian, Richard G. *The Armenian Genocide in Perspective.* New Brunswick, New Jersey: Transaction Books, 1986.

Katz, Zeu, (et al.), eds. *Handbook of Major Soviet Nationalities.* New York: The Free Press, 1975.

Los Angeles Times, Dec. 19, 1988, Jan. 13, 1989, April 21, 1989, July 23, 1989.

Nalbandian, Louise. *The Armenian Revolutionary Movement: The Development of Armenian Political Parties through the Nineteenth Century.* Berkeley: University of California Press, 1963.

The New York Times, Dec. 12, 1988, Dec. 16, 1988: A1.

Reader's Digest, March 1989.

Wall Street Journal, Dec. 9, 1988.

The Washington Post, Dec. 9, 1988.

Index

The Author, Chris Engholm, is the author of several books on Asia. He travels frequently in Asia and resides in Del Mar, California.

Illustrations designed by Maurie Manning capture the drama of the events described in this book.

Manning majored in illustration at Massachusetts College of Art in Boston and has been a professional children's illustrator for more than six years. Her work appears regularly in such magazines as *Children's Digest, Humpty Dumpty,* and *Highlights for Children.*

Manning was assisted by a team of three artists: Michael Spackman, Robert Caldwell, and Randol Eagles. A professional painter for more than nineteen years, Michael Spackman received his training at the High Museum Academy of Art in Atlanta. Robert Caldwell, a graduate of Syracuse University with a degree in fine arts, has been a fine arts professional for eight years. Randol Eagles is a specialist in figurative illustration, and has been a professional illustrator for three years.

Special thanks to Pamela Lopez Johnson for research and interviews, and to Alice Fundukian of the Armenian National Committee for her insights, advice, and guidance.